Lyric

Riffs

2nd Edition

Other Books by Dave:

Top Stories – 31 parables retold with contemporary comments

Pulp Gospel – 31 bits of the Bible retold with comments

Film & Faith – 66 movie clips that bring the Bible to life, with questions and comments

Parables - A collection of stories to chew on. Yarns with an eye on another world

Sons of Thunder – A contemporary gospel

No More Heroes – Cain, Solomon & Jacob in a modern tale of men, women, dads and crime

Diary of a Wimpy Christian – Humorous and honest reflections on life, faith and bumbling along

The Shed – A novel. 40 days in a shed with a disgruntled guy, and the pilgrims, stragglers and wanderers he encounters

The Twelfth Seer – A novel. A big screen, action adventure; the quest for divine power

Dave is a freelance speaker and author. For more info and to receive his regular creative emails –
davehopwood.com

Lyrical

2nd Edition

Readings based on Bible verses.

Riff: a repeated. arresting. short. memorable. recurring phrase that drives and affects the whole piece.

List of Riffs

1. Flesh
2. Today
3. The People's Prayer
4. Free?
5. New Genesis
6. Always Will
7. Touch Wood
8. Thirteen
9. Hanging On
10. Lives of Contradiction
11. The Call
12. Jesus Wept
13. Finishing
14. It Is Finished
15. Sow Far
16. Thirsty
17. Wherever
18. An Update?
19. For Those
20. Shepherd
21. My Unbelief
22. Open Invitation
23. My God
24. Christmas List 1
25. Christmas List 2
26. Christmas List 3
27. Light
28. A Time for Everything
29. He Set My Feet...
30. Questions
31. Upon This
32. King of Shocks
33. Purpose
34. With Those
35. Lead Us
36. Shine
37. Stand
38. Vision
39. Prayer 91
40. Plans

List of Riffs (continued)

41. John 21
42. Beatitude
43. For All the April Fools
44. Nothing
45. Outward
46. Bodies
47. Voter's Prayer
48. Praise 150
49. Feet
50. Ascension
51. The Helper
52. Who
53. I Am
54. Follow Me
55. A-Z
56. Embracing
57. Valley
58. Surely
59. Blessing
60. Money-love
61. Movie
62. Waters
63. In Vain
64. Why?
65. Encouragement
66. Blessed
67. Is
68. Honour
69. No One
70. Days
71. In Him
72. Believe
73. Speaking
74. Sheep
75. Excuses
76. Resurrection 1 & 2
77. Boast
78. Living Letters
79. Closer
80. God

81.	Confession	102.	Treasure
82.	Beginnings	103.	When
83.	Dust	104.	Prepare the Way…
84.	Kingdom	105.	139
85.	Abandoned	106.	Love Is
86.	Bitter/Sweet	107.	Presence
87.	Depths	108.	No Longer Despised
88.	Sustenance	109.	Minders
89.	Seeking	110.	Help
90.	Rescue	111.	Longing
91.	The Peace of God	112.	Shelter
92.	My Spirit Rejoices	113.	Doves, Ravens…
93.	Love, Walk, Live	114.	The One
94.	Loaves	115.	Former Things
95.	XOXO	116.	Fresh Start
96.	Praise!	117.	Bread and Wine
97.	Mindful of Us	118.	The Bible
98.	OMG	119.	Chosen
99.	Comfort	120.	Psalm 51
100.	Salvation	121.	PTL
101.	My Sheep	122.	In Disguise

1. *Flesh*

And so God became flesh

And lived amongst us

He became flesh

And played in the street

He became flesh

And was one of many local lads called Joshua

He became flesh

And learnt his dad's skills

He became flesh

And sweated to keep the family business going

He became flesh

And was taxed to the hilt by the Romans

He became flesh

Had favourite food, good friends and rings under his eyes

And so God became flesh

And loved telling funny stories

He became flesh

And was popular in the neighbourhood

He became flesh

And had a cousin who had gone wild

He became flesh

Slipped out of town one day and returned with a manifesto for life

God became flesh

And understands suffering, temptation, hope, despair, laughter, anguish, craving, fear, satisfaction and doubt.

John 1 v 14

2. *Today*

As a man dies naked, vulnerable and rejected,

He looks at the figure fading beside him and mutters the line

Today you will be with me in paradise

Then he turns to the beggar breathing his last in the gutter

Today you will be with me in paradise

To the drug addict who fell into addiction to escape her past

Today you will be with me in paradise

To the pensioner dying alone at home

Today you will be with me in paradise

To the husband beaten and dying outside the pub in the early hours

Today you will be with me in paradise

To the child whose short life has been used up by others

Today you will be with me in paradise

To the forgotten and the lonely, the unlovely and non-celebrities

Today you will be with me in paradise

To the failures and the discarded ones

Today you will be with me in paradise

To the frightened, the weak and the small
Today you will be with me in paradise.

Luke 23 v 43

3. *The People's Prayer*

A man on a corner lifts his head to the sky,
his blank face speaking silently

Our father, in heaven

A teenager sucks on a cigarette and blows
the smoke to the heavens

May your name be honoured

A worker who wouldn't dare be too vocal
about his beliefs fingers the cross in his ear

Your kingdom come, your will be done

A group of soldiers rebuild a school that's
been recently bombed out

On earth as it is in heaven

A college girl pays triple for a copy of The Big
Issue

Give us this day our daily bread

He bites his lip and shakes his head with
regret

And forgive us for the things we do wrong

She jabs the keys on her mobile phone,
framing the apology in her mind

As we forgive those who do wrong to us

A bus queue of agnostics send up silent cries
for help about the coming day

For yours is the kingdom, the power and the glory

She watches the clock as another difficult afternoon finally closes

Forever and ever, Amen.

Matthew 6 vv 9-13

4. *Free?*

The truth'll set me free

But it may upset me first

The truth'll set me free

But it may not be too tidy

The truth'll set me free

Though it may divert my plans

The truth'll set me free

But it most likely won't scan too well or rhyme neatly or go the way I expect.

John 8 v 32

5. *New Genesis*

In the beginning was the word

When the universe was merely a glint in the designer's eye

In the beginning was the word

When he swept his hand before him and gathered potential in his fist

In the beginning was the word

As the whole of creation crowded out the corners of his mind

In the beginning was the word

When he spoke and every single speck of dust and every glimmer of light tumbled from his lips

In the beginning was the word

As worlds were born and galaxies formed

In the beginning was the word

As seas roared, volcanoes spluttered and skies bled with shocking sunsets

In the beginning was the word

And juggernaut creatures plastered their articulated footprints across the earth

In the beginning was the word

And people found a home and settled in Eden

In the beginning was the word

As the designer rested and folks took up their brand new responsibilities

In the beginning was the word

As Adam invented lawlessness and his son Cain created homicide

In the beginning was the word

And it became flesh and moved in with Adam and Cain and you and I

In the beginning was the word

And the word gave up his last breath for the old creation and in doing so began the work of making it *new*.

John 1 v 1

6. *Always Will*

God so loved the cosmos

That he didn't sit on his hands and sigh

God so loved the cosmos

That he didn't organise an enquiry

God so loved the cosmos

That he didn't look for someone to blame

God so loved the cosmos

That he didn't crack cynical jokes about it

God so loved the cosmos

That he didn't bury his head in the sand

God so loved the cosmos

That he didn't go drinking or shopping or watch films to escape the pain

God so loved the cosmos

That he sent his only son, his beloved boy, to live, laugh, walk, talk, heal, cure, agonise, argue, debate, wrestle, encourage, cry, groan, smile, listen, ponder, tell stories, confront kangaroo justice, experience pain, suffer, die, rise from the dead, draw in the sand, write good news in the dirt, cook on a beach, forgive the betrayal of others, sit in the gutter, look for the lost and love the unlovable

God so loved the cosmos

That he invited everyone to trust in that boy
who, in such a short time, did so much for so
many

God so loved the cosmos

And he always will.

John 3 v 16

7. *Touch Wood*

Touch Wood - it might be lucky
Touch Wood - you'll be okay
Touch Wood - it's just tradition
Touch Wood - could change the day

He *touched wood* for all of us
Touched wood with the backs of both his hands
Touched wood, no luck on Golgotha
Touched wood and bled for lives and lands

Not the sheen of polished table
Two beams crossed and lifted high
No quick fix, or magic there
The tree maker, *touching wood* to die

Touch Wood - you can still see him now
Touch Wood - round necks, in ears, on walls
Touch Wood - one man on the tree of life
Touch Wood - nailed up there, once for all.

Colossians 1 vv 18-22

8. *Thirteen*

Thirteen - the number of gloom
Thirteen - the digits of dread
Thirteen - the Friday to be avoided
Thirteen – better left unsaid

13 round that table
13 so the good book said
13 not unlucky but planned
13 and two will soon be dead

13 - he wouldn't avoid that Friday
13 - submerged himself in dread
13 - took on the mantle of gloom
13 and 12 left him for dead

13 went down in history
13 a bad night's work they say
But if the truth be ever told
Sunday would wash *13* away.

Matthew 26 vv 2-28

9. *Hanging On*

I waited patiently for the Lord
He leant forward and heard my cry
I waited patiently for the Lord
And I'm waiting still
I waited patiently for the Lord
And my patience is running thin
I waited patiently for the Lord
It's like queueing forever on a wet Monday
I waited patiently for the Lord
Like a tunnel with no end in sight
I waited patiently for the Lord
And I'm not the person I used to be
I waited patiently for the Lord
It's a long, infuriating experience
I waited patiently for the Lord
I've given up thirteen times but I'm back
again
I waited patiently for the Lord
I've nowhere else to go
I waited patiently for the Lord
Though I'm fading fast now
I waited patiently for the Lord

And now I know what waiting and patience
are all about

I waited patiently for the Lord

And then I waited impatiently, and then I just
sat there

And at an unexpected moment

He leant forward and heard my cry.

Psalm 40

10. *Lives of Contradiction*

The truth will set you free
We have mixed motives
The truth will set you free
We're heroes and villains
The truth will set you free
Forgiving and critical
The truth will set you free
Cowards and trailblazers
The truth will set you free
Motivated and demotivated
The truth will set you free
Often saintly and sinful
The truth will set you free
Selfish and selfless
The truth will set you free
A mix of integrity and hypocrisy
The truth will set you free
Selfless and selfish
The truth will set you free
Convicted yet acquitted.

John 8 v 32

11. *The Call*

She met him
At a funeral
At a wedding
While fetching water
He said 'Follow me'

He met him out fishing
In a tax office
Leaning against a tree
He said 'Follow me'

I met him on Twitter
On the internet
In the cinema
He said 'Follow me'

She met him in a city bar
In a country pub
In the library
He said 'Follow me'
We see him on the sports field
In the High Street
In the gutter
He says 'Follow me'

They see him
She meets him
He spots him
I bump into him
He says 'Follow me'

I met him in a Good Book
He said 'Follow me'
He met him on a dying cross
He said 'Follow me'
She met him in the light of dawn
He said 'Follow me'
They see him every day
He says 'Follow me'.

Mark 8 vv 34-36

12. *Jesus Wept*

Jesus Wept

As I played with my riches

As others sat in squalor

As the slaves toiled and suffered

As the planet writhed in pain

Jesus Wept

And it was all too raw

I was so embarrassed

As his tears cried a river

And the river burst its banks

Jesus Wept

And the deluge eroded my defences

His compassion assaulted my dry eyes

He wouldn't quit, wouldn't stop

No matter how high I piled the sandbags

Jesus Wept

And went on weeping, doing his best to get my attention.

John 11 v 35; Luke 5 v 16

13. *Finishing*

It is finished

The words echo in his mind as he steps into the dawn from the shifting shadows in that cave

It is finished

The words ring through history echoed in a billion lives laid down for others

It is finished

The words reverberate through the living of those who right now are making small differences

It is finished

The words that herald a new start for so many who thought they'd reached a dead end

It will be finished

There'll be a day when the finishing will end. And the never-ending will kick in...

John 19 v 30

14. *It Is Finished*

Though it feels far from done
It is finished
Though the battle's far from won
It is finished
Though the struggles still rage on
It is finished
Though this planet's nearly done

It is finished
Though I've long-since had enough
It is finished
Though the road is way too rough
It is finished
Though the rich have too much stuff
It is finished
And we've really had enough

It is finished
Another dawn is breaking
It is finished
This world no longer cracked and breaking
It is finished
Mankind no longer sore and aching

It is finished

There'll be no more sham and faking

It will be finished

And 'it is finished' will have no meaning any more.

John 19 v 30

15. *Sow Far*

A farmer went out to sow some seeds
Some fell amongst thorns
Some fell on the hard path
Some fell among thistles
Some fell on good soil
Some fell on bad
Some fell on deaf ears
Some fell in churches
Some fell in pubs
Some fell in graveyards
Some fell in schoolyards

Some fell in homes... on the streets... in
workplaces... sports fields... TV studios...
office blocks... labourers' yards...
motorways... supermarkets...
colleges... coffee shops...

A farmer went out to sow some seeds

And some found good ground, began to grow
and bore an awful lot of fruit

Some didn't.

Matthew 13 vv 3-9

16. *Thirsty*

He's offered vinegar on a stick

Panacea for the pain

But he still thirsts

His throat is parched as he sees the past

His mouth is dry as he tastes the present

And he still thirsts

He turns to the man beside him and offers a promise

He sees his mother and offers her hope

Yet he still thirsts

While there is a world turning and people calling

Whilst tyrants rise and the innocent fall

He thirsts

And no vinegar on a stick

No platitudal panacea

Can quench the longing

For justice, peace and reconciliation

He thirsts.

John 19 v 2-29

17. *Wherever*

Though you walk through the valley of shadows

I will be with you wherever you go

When you lay down in perfect peace

I will be with you wherever you go

When you're laughing, dancing, crying, sulking

I will be with you wherever you go

When you find a reason to get up in the morning, and when you don't

I will be with you wherever you go

When you consider yourself a good person, and when you don't

I will be with you wherever you go

When you feel spiritual and when you don't

I will be with you wherever you go

When you want to be near me, and when you don't

I will be with you wherever you go

When you give up and vent your anger on me

I will be with you wherever you go

When you look up and smile

I will be with you wherever you go

When you ignore other people

I will be with you wherever you go

And when you do every little thing you can to help them

I will be with you wherever you go

In the dark, in the light, in the rain and the sun

I will be with you wherever you go

When you can find me, and when you can't

I will be with you wherever you go.

Joshua 1 v 9; Genesis 28 v 15; Deuteronomy 31 v 8

18. *An Update?*

He could rewrite the story

Not be so vulnerable

He could rewrite the story

Not appear as a child

He could rewrite the story

Not have to work hard with his dad

He could rewrite the story

Not live in an oppressed country

He could rewrite the story

Not clash with the religious authorities or powerful elite

He could rewrite the story

Not spend so much time with the poor, the dirty and the sick

He could rewrite the story

Not open himself up to so much ridicule, flak and criticism

He could rewrite the story

Not sweat blood in that garden of dark loneliness

He could rewrite the story

Not feel the pounding horror of those nails

He could rewrite the story

Not die alone

He could rewrite the story

Not turn the world upside down on one stone
shuffling morning

He could rewrite the story

Not invite people to share in that same
difficult way

He could rewrite it, remake the film, update
the play

Turn back time and take a wider road

Delete the difficult bits

He could rewrite the story

He considered it in his worst, isolated
moments

But he won't

This timeless classic stands, the print fixed,
the storybook splayed open

No rewrite.

Mark 14 v 36; John 12 vv 27-28

19. *For Those*

Being accused of eating with scum, Jesus replied,

'I didn't come to call the righteous...

But to call the sinners and

For those who are sick

For those not very spiritual

For those not too rich

For those none too happy

For those who are oppressed

For those who are up against it

Those who wrestle with doubt

Those who are unpopular

The non-celebrities

The ordinary

The plain

The lost.'

Mark 2 vv 15-17

20. *Shepherd*

The LORD is my shepherd

My satnav, my personal trainer, my president, my prime minister, my mentor

I have everything I need.

I want plenty of things, crave so much, desire a world of pleasure

He lets me rest in green meadows; he leads me beside peaceful streams.

I dream of a break, somewhere to get away from it all, a place of R&R

He renews my strength.

I'm so tired sometimes, so wrung out from my day, so desperate for some space

He guides me along right paths, bringing honour to his name.

I get lost, we all get lost, blind alleys wait like predators

Even when I walk through the dark valley of evil, I will not be afraid,

The news is always bad, the world can seem a crumbling sphere, its people bent on self-harm

For you are close beside me. Your rod and your staff protect and comfort me.

Popular opinion informs me that there is nothing out there, that we're a clever accident

You prepare a feast for me in the presence of my enemies.

Enemies in many guises wait to capsize us - peer pressure, cynicism, undermining rebuffs

You welcome me as a guest, anointing my head with oil.

Dark corners of rejection litter the place, closed doors, sharp rebuffs, corners of lonely solitude

My cup overflows with blessings. Surely your goodness and love will pursue me forever

So many things are temporary, the years fly, and the pleasures are fleeting

I will live in the presence of the LORD all my days

One day... one day...

Psalm 23

21. *My Unbelief*

When I see half the picture, but not the whole

I believe, help me in my unbelief

When I'm angry and disappointed

I believe, help me in my unbelief

When I fear I've made no difference

I believe, help me in my unbelief

When I feel like the odd one out

I believe, help me in my unbelief

When everyone else seems so sure of themselves

I believe, help me in my unbelief

When friends are hard to find

I believe, help me in my unbelief

When life is another series of uphill climbs

I believe, help me in my unbelief

When I just don't have it in me to keep going

I believe, help me in my unbelief.

Mark 9 v 24

22. *Open Invitation*

Come all who are thirsty
All who are weary and worried
Come all who are thirsty
All who are bleary and bored
Come all who are thirsty
Those who know they are spiritually poor
Come all who are thirsty
Those who are tired of spin
Come all who are thirsty
Those who are parched for peace
Come all who are thirsty
Those who wrestle with themselves and their schemes
Come all who are thirsty
Those who wrestle with the world and its grand designs
Come all who are thirsty
And you will find living water
And sustaining food
Eternal and free
Come all who are thirsty
Come and buy
For free.

Isaiah 55 v 1; John 4 v 14; Matthew 11 v 28

23. *My God*

A man hangs on the horizon, his body tearing on nails

His soul immersed in lonely agony; his voice cracking as he whispers:

My God my God why have you forsaken me?

For every dark moment since the planet started spinning

My God my God why have you forsaken me?

For every broken heart and tortured spirit

My God my God why have you forsaken me?

For every lost soul and empty future

My God my God why have you forsaken me?

For everything that rails against true humanity

My God my God why have you forsaken me?

For every person subject to the twisted whims of dictatorship

My God my God why have you forsaken me?

For every silent believer in a world of vocal oppression

My God my God why have you forsaken me?

For every lost memory of a future and a hope

My God my God why have you forsaken me?

For the unresolved nature of Sunday's resurrection

My God my God why have you forsaken me…

Matthew 27 v 46

24. *Christmas List*

*The people who walked in darkness have seen
a great light*

In the crying of a baby

*The people who walked in darkness have seen
a great light*

In the signature of a star

*The people who walked in darkness have seen
a great light*

In the surround sound from the sky

*The people who walked in darkness have seen
a great light*

In the stories of the first followers

*The people who walked in darkness have seen
a great light*

In the history of two thousand years

*The people who walked in darkness have seen
a great light*

In the tales from the pubs and pulpits

*The people who walked in darkness have seen
a great light*

In the prophets on the street corners

*The people who walked in darkness have seen
a great light*

In the carols, hymns and songs

The people who walked in darkness have seen a great light

In the videos on YouTube

The people who walked in darkness have seen a great light

In the pain and the trouble of these days

The people who walked in darkness have seen a great light

In the gloom and the uncertainty of these nights

The people who walked in darkness have seen a great light

Beyond the glitter and the tinsel of this hallowed, stressful time

The people who walked in darkness have seen a great light.

Isaiah 9 v 2

25. *Christmas List 2*

In the words of the wise men from the east

'Where's the king of the Jews? We've come to worship him.'

And those from the north and the south and the west

'Where's the king of the Jews? We've come to worship him.'

In the words of the wise women down the ages

'Where's the king of the Jews? We've come to worship him.'

And the children with their simple trust

'Where's the king of the Jews? We've come to worship him.'

The old who've lived their faithful lives

'Where's the king of the Jews? We've come to worship him.'

The priests who've served through good and bad

'Where's the king of the Jews? We've come to worship him.'

The confused that hoped for something better

'Where's the king of the Jews? We've come to worship him.'

The agnostics who want to believe but struggle

'Where's the king of the Jews? We've come to worship him.'

The disheartened that lost their faith on the way

'Where's the king of the Jews? We've come to worship him.'

The prodigals, the rebels, the angry young things

'Where's the king of the Jews? We've come to worship him.'

The grumpy, the guilty, the regretful and ragged

'Where's the king of the Jews? We've come to worship him.'

The cry of so many secret pilgrims down the years

'Where's the king of the Jews? We've come to worship him.'

Matthew 2 v2

26. *Christmas List 3*

As the old man looked into those tiny eyes he knew, the waiting was over…

'This child will be the falling and rising of many…'

He has hung around a long time for this moment

'This child will be the falling and rising of many…'

Endured long nights and lonely days

'This child will be the falling and rising of many…'

He's prayed, hoped, doubted, trusted, battered the ceiling with his cries

'This child will be the falling and rising of many…'

And now at last he holds the fragile answer in his arms

'This child will be the falling and rising of many…'

The wide eyed, vulnerable way forward for the world

'This child will be the falling and rising of many…'

And in an instant he knew the terrible, wonderful, life-giving, heartbreaking truth

'This child will be the falling and rising of many...'

This is only the beginning... there will be many more waiting in the wings...

'This child will be the falling and rising of many...'

The rich cannot go on exploiting the poor

'This child will be the falling and rising of many...'

The powerful will not always hold sway

'This child will be the falling and rising of many...'

Dishevelled shepherds, out watching their flocks, will visit this king

'This child will be the falling and rising of many...'

Dominant, child-murdering tyrants will crumble and fade

'This child will be the falling and rising of many...'

Ordinary fisherman, prostitutes and tax collectors will rise

'This child will be the falling and rising of many...'

The power-broking elite will diminish

'This child will be the falling and rising of many…'

The little people will be lifted – and the proud will disappear

'This child will be the falling and rising of many…'

And one day the waiting for justice will be no more…

Luke 2 v 34

27. *Light*

There's a strange glow in the sky
A light penetrating the darkness
Calling to a young girl and a carpenter
Singing to dishevelled shepherds
Leading distant mystics
Travelling down the years
Still burning bright
The light penetrating the darkness
And the darkness battling hard
But never overcoming it.

John 1 v 5

28. *A Time for Everything*

There is a time for everything.

A time to work and a time to play.

A time to talk and a time to listen.

A time to laugh and - yes - a time to cry.

A time to be cool and a time to be honest.

A time to be happy and a time to complain.

A time to rush and a time to wait.

A time for TV and a time for reality.

A time for loud music and a time for quiet.

A time to mess about and a time to knuckle down.

A time to respect, never a time to disrespect.

A time to chill and a time to get up at 6.00am.

A time to encourage and a time to be encouraged.

Ecclesiastes 3 v 1-8

29. *He Set My Feet Upon a Rock*

He set my feet upon a rock and made my footsteps firm

Sometimes the rock seems as hard as granite

Solidly immovable, a sure foundation in the regular storms

He set my feet upon a rock and made my footsteps firm

At other times it feels like shifting sand

Like walking on water, my steps restless, unpredictable

He set my feet upon a rock and made my footsteps firm

There are days when it seems smooth and restful, a place to stop and ease my mind

And there are days when it's uncomfortable, urging me on, prodding me to keep moving

He set my feet upon a rock and made my footsteps firm

Sometimes this rock seems unbreakable, the most reliable substance in the universe

At other times it feels so fragile, so tender, like brittle, wafer-thin ice

He set my feet upon a rock and made my footsteps firm

So I remind myself - it's a rock that has stood the tests of time, fashion and pressure

A global foundation, spanning history and the tides of restless humanity

He set my feet upon a rock and made my footsteps firm

And though I often feel small and insignificant

And my perception of the rock ebbs and flows

I stretch the muscles of my faith, and reach for those well-trodden phrases once again

He set my feet upon a rock and made my footsteps firm; many will see and put their trust in him.

Psalm 40 v 2

30. *Questions*

What good is it to win the world and lose your soul?

How can I enter the kingdom?

What is truth?

Where are the masts these days? Where do we nail our colours?

Why do you call me good, no one is good except God?

So what are you saying about the humble, unremarkable, non-celebrity from Nazareth?

How long oh Lord, how long?

Lord, when did we ever see you thirsty and give you something to drink?

Are you the king of the Jews?

What must I do to be saved?

Why do the nations rage?

Lord, when did we ever see you hungry and feed you?

How long must I be with you until you believe?

My God, why have you forsaken me?

Why are you looking for the living amongst the dead?

31. *Upon This*

Upon this rock I will build my church

Upon this wayward bunch of arguing disciples

Upon this rock I will build my church

Upon these small, struggling New Testament churches

Upon this rock I will build my church

Upon these believers who are still sorting out their theology

Upon this rock I will build my church

Upon these ministers doing their best to lead fragile flocks

Upon this rock I will build my church

Upon these individuals wrestling to form a community

Upon this rock I will build my church

Upon these doubters, renegades, failures and frauds

Upon this rock I will build my church

Upon those whom the world forgets

Upon this rock I will build my church

Those that society counts as down and out

Upon this rock I will build my church

Upon those willing to lay everything on the line

Upon this rock I will build my church
Upon anyone willing to give it a go
Upon this rock I will build my church
Upon you.

Matthew 16 v 18

32. *King of Shocks*

Time and again he shakes them up
'Love your enemies
Woe to the rich
Let the children come to me'

Time and again he shakes them up
'God is with the poor, the grieving, the humble
She's not dead, she's sleeping
You feed them'

Time and again he shakes them up
'Your sins are forgiven
I am the resurrection
One of you will betray me'

Time and again he shakes them up
'I don't call you servants, I call you friends
Unless you become like little children
Give to Caesar's what's Caesar's, to God what
is God's'

Time and again he shakes them up
Pulls the rug, flips their worldview
'I'm going to be killed
Three days later I'll be back

I'll be with you always.'

33. *Purpose*

Is there a purpose to all this?

Time comes around and goes around

We are born and we die

We plant food and we pull it up again, we grow it, we waste it, we eat it

We fight and get injured, we kill and we hurt, we patch ourselves up and hope to heal

We break things down and we rebuild them, we tear them down and build again

We laugh and we cry, we mourn and we celebrate

We collect things and we scatter them again, we hoard and we give away and we hoard again

We buy things and we get rid of them, we pay and we consume

We tear things and we fix them, we damage and we patch up

We keep silent and we speak up, our words go round and round

We love, we hate, we adore, we argue, we go to war and we make peace

Time passes, the days fly, things rise and fall, we come and we go

There is a time for everything. But is there a purpose? And who gives these things meaning?

Ecclesiastes 3 v 1-8

34. *With Those*

God is *with those* who know they need him
God is *with those* who hearts are breaking
God is *with those* who are humble and gentle
With those who long for justice and truth
With those who are compassionate
Those who aim for purity
Those who work for peace
Those who are persecuted, put down,
overlooked, lied about and marginalised
because of Jesus.

For God himself experienced these things
Knowing his need
His heart repeatedly broken
The humble, gentle king
Longing for truth and justice
The compassionate son
Full of grace and purity
Working for peace
And ultimately persecuted, put down,
overlooked, lied about and marginalised.

Matthew 5 v 1-12

35. *Lead Us*

Lead us not into temptation

Keep us from false guilt and the burden of self-loathing

Lead us not into temptation

Save us from pride, arrogance, and the quick-witted judging of others

Lead us not into temptation

Take us away from the notion that we have all the answers

Lead us not into temptation

Open our eyes to the world as you see it

Lead us not into temptation

Soften our hearts where they harden on a daily basis

Lead us not into temptation

Steer us away from unnecessary argument and snappy put downs

Lead us not into temptation

Guide us away from the places of arrogance and lack of respect

Lead us not into temptation

Into a place of truth, compassion and grace

Lead us not into temptation

Take us with you Jesus, where you'll walk today.   ***Matthew 6 v 13***

36. *Shine*

Let your light shine before people
Never tire of passing on that smile
Let your light shine before people
Offering that kind word
Let your light shine before people
Apologising for those mistakes
Let your light shine before people
Encouraging the also-rans
Let your light shine before people
Setting humility above pride
Let your light shine before people
Challenging the frequent injustice
Let your light shine before people
Working for peace and reconciliation
Let your light shine before people
Being a sign of hope and restoration
Let your light shine before people
So that they may praise your father in
heaven.

Matthew 5 v 16

37. *Stand*

*Stand at the crossroads and look; ask for the
ancient paths, ask where the good way is,
and walk in it*

Take a breather, just a second or two

*Stand at the crossroads and look; ask for the
ancient paths, ask where the good way is,
and walk in it*

**Take a coffee break, go outside, look to the
skies**

*Stand at the crossroads and look; ask for the
ancient paths, ask where the good way is,
and walk in it*

**Pause in the busyness of the day, in the
stress and the angst**

*Stand at the crossroads and look; ask for the
ancient paths, ask where the good way is,
and walk in it*

**Look around, see the signs, listen to the
voices and the sighs**

*Stand at the crossroads and look; ask for the
ancient paths, ask where the good way is,
and walk in it*

**Talk to me, about the struggles, about the
kind of help you need**

*Stand at the crossroads and look; ask for the
ancient paths, ask where the good way is,
and walk in it*

Open the book when you get a chance, see if the words come to life, if they spill off the page
Stand at the crossroads and look; ask for the ancient paths, ask where the good way is, and walk in it
and you will find rest for your souls.

Jeremiah 6 v 16

38. *Vision*

withou
tvisionpeop
lefallapart. Unle
ssyoubecomelikealit
tlechildyoucannotseethe
kingdomofGod. Unlessyouarefai
thfulinsmallermattersyouwon'tbef
aithfulinlargeones. Whoeverwan
tstolead mustbeaservanttoothers.

Proverbs 29 v 18; Matthew 18 v 3
Luke 16 v 10; Matthew 22 v 26

39. *Prayer 91*

You are my God in you I trust
Though I fear the darkness
You are my God in you I trust
Though the future is unknown
You are my God in you I trust
Though I'm under pressure to doubt you
You are my God in you I trust
Though guilt often ambushes me
You are my God in you I trust
Though sorrow drags me down
You are my God in you I trust
Though the unexpected lies in wait
You are my God in you I trust
Though others are not easy
You are my God in you I trust
In you alone I find my refuge,
You are my God in you I trust
You're my place of safety
You are my God in you I trust.

Psalm 91

40. *Plans*

We make our plans but God has the last word
Life so often surprises me
We make our plans but God has the last word
I say I'll do this, that and the other

We make our plans but God has the last word
I expect the day to pan out in a certain way
We make our plans but God has the last word
It twists and turns like a country lane
We make our plans but God has the last word
Slips from my grasp like a piece of soap
We make our plans but God has the last word
Roads close unexpectedly and diversions crop up

We make our plans but God has the last word
I smile out of the blue, laugh without prior warning
We make our plans but God has the last word
My heart breaks when I least expect it
We make our plans but God has the last word
I'm moved to help when I should be rushing on

We make our plans but God has the last word
I find myself being flexible when I want to be stubborn

We make our plans but God has the last word
The one constant seems to be change
We make our plans but God has the last word.

Proverbs 16 v 9

41. *John 21*

I sink when I walk on water
And still he beckons saying 'Follow me'
I fear getting things wrong
And still he beckons saying 'Follow me'
I'm overcautious and reticent
And still he beckons saying 'Follow me'
Preoccupied with my past mistakes
And still he beckons saying 'Follow me'
I think about the times of letting him down
And still he beckons saying 'Follow me'
Times of burying my head in the sand
And still he beckons saying 'Follow me'
I'm conflicted and reluctant
And still he beckons saying 'Follow me'
Can be so easily double-minded and two-faced
And still he beckons saying 'Follow me'
I'm really not up to the job
And still he beckons saying 'Follow me'
He'd do better sending someone else
And still he beckons saying 'Follow me'.

Luke 5 v 27

42. *Beatitude*

He sat down on a hill one day and reassured them:

Blessed are you... (or in other words) - God is with you...

In the hard places. Which was a shock for they had been told otherwise.

Blessed are you... God is with you

In the tricky moments, in the difficulties and doubts

God is with you

When you can't find a reason to believe

God is with you

When you are doubting, questioning, searching

God is with you

When you are the only one speaking up

God is with you

When you can see the emperor has no clothes

God is with you

When no one else is listening

God is with you

When you're standing up for the right

God is with you

When you're telling your story from the heart

God is with you

Though you are shouted down and pushed

aside
God is with you
When you walk that second mile, and your
feet are bleeding
God is with you
When you know that neither gold nor silver
will ever make you truly rich
God is with you
When you are full, empty, rich, poor, lost or
found.
God is with you
In the moments and the days, in the darkness
and the light.

Matthew 5 v 3-12

43. *For All the April Fools*

God chose the foolish things to confound the wise

If it all goes wrong today

God chose the foolish things to confound the wise

If you end up putting both feet in your mouth

God chose the foolish things to confound the wise

Tripping over your own clumsiness

God chose the foolish things to confound the wise

Stubbing your emotional toes

God chose the foolish things to confound the wise

Putting your foot in it again

God chose the foolish things to confound the wise

Looking the idiot

God chose the foolish things to confound the wise

Feeling small

God chooses you.

1 Corinthians 1 v 27

44. *Nothing*

Nothing can separate us from the love of God
Death can't, and life can't
The angels can't, and the demons can't
Our fears for today, our worries about tomorrow
Even the powers of hell can't keep God's love away
New discoveries nor ancient legends

Barbed humour nor cynical put-downs
Political parties nor government legislation

No individuals, groups, countries or continents
No personal troubles or personality defects

High above the sky or in the deepest ocean
Walking on the moon or stranded on the sea bed
Nothing in all creation will ever be able to separate us
From the love of God that is revealed in Christ Jesus our Lord.

Romans 8 vv 38-39

45. *Outward*

We may look at the outward appearance

the clothes, size, age, fashion, shape

but God looks at the heart

the courage, humility and compassion

the patience, kindness and faithfulness

We may look at the outward appearance

the hair, sex, fame, popularity, good looks

but God looks at the heart

the faith, hope, love

the hunger for justice, the thirst for truth

We may judge by outward appearances,
quickly and harshly, we can't help it

He judges the whole person with fairness and
integrity, he can't help it.

1 Samuel 17 v 6

46. *Bodies*

When I was a child, I talked like a child, I thought like a child, I reasoned like a child

When I was a teenager, I talked like a teenager, I thought like a teenager, I reasoned like a teenager

When I was strong, I talked like a strong person, I thought like a strong person, I reasoned like a strong person

When I was an adult, I talked like an adult, I thought like an adult, I reasoned like an adult

As I grew older, I talked like an older person, I thought like an older person, I reasoned like an older person

As I grew weaker, I talked like a weaker person, I thought like a weaker person, I reasoned like a weaker person

So it is with Christ's body. We are many parts, and we all belong to each other.

1 Corinthians 12 vv 12-13; 1 Corinthians 13 v 11

47. *Voter's Prayer*

Lord,

we pray for your guidance and wisdom as we consider who to vote for in the coming elections. We pray for our leaders, that their hearts and minds will be tuned towards the people, rather than only benefitting themselves. We pray that integrity, justice and mercy might be the watchwords and priorities of these political campaigns. We pray for honesty and transparency, and for men and women who might lead by example, so that we may be challenged and inspired to follow their lead. Please help us to have wisdom and insight as we battle to discern the best way forward. Open our hearts and minds, our wills and consciences to your worldview.

In Jesus' name, amen.

Micah 6 v 8; 1 Timothy 2 vv 1-2

48. *Praise 150*

Praise the Lord.
Praise him with a blast of the trumpet;
Praise him with the lyre and harp!
Praise him with the tambourine, rapping and
dancing;
Praise him with stringed instruments, pan
pipes and flutes!
Praise him with the beat of drums and the
clash of cymbals;
Praise him with the whisper of silence;
Praise him with the hush of stillness.
Praise him with walking, talking, hurrying,
slowing down.
Praise him as we watch, get involved, pray,
give and offer a hand.
Praise him in the street, in the cinema,
church and pub;
Praise him at home, at work, at the school
and job centre.
Praise him.
Any place. Any time. Everywhere.

Psalm 150

49. *Feet*

How lovely on the mountains are the feet of those

Who bring good news

How lovely on the pavements are the feet of those

Who step into the shoes of others

How lovely in the shadows are the feet of those

Who are prepared to walk in the difficult places

How lovely on the rough ground are the feet of those

Who bring relief and a way forward

How lovely in the undergrowth are the feet of those

Who step into the unknown to pave a new path

How lovely in the unknown places are the feet of those

Who make small sacrifices to change the world

How lovely in the dull places are the feet of those

Who do the same ordinary things time after time for the sake of someone else

How lovely on the mountains, on the rough ground and on the pavements
In the shadows, dull places, undergrowth and unknown places

Are the feet of him
Who brings good news
One who lives it, dies for it and returns to guide us in his way.

Isaiah 52 v 7; Romans 10 v 15

50. *Ascension*

I will not leave you as orphans
Alone in a world of trouble
I will not leave you as orphans
Though you may not always see me
I will not leave you as orphans
I'll be with you always, every day
I will not leave you as orphans
You may feel lonely, but you won't be alone
I will not leave you as orphans
I will be with you.

John 14 v 18

51. *The Helper*

When the helper comes he'll guide you into all truth

About life, the world and its priorities

When the helper comes he'll guide you into all truth

About the past, the present and the future

When the helper comes he'll guide you into all truth

About hope, justice and freedom

When the helper comes he'll guide you into all truth

About people, compassion and forgiveness

When the helper comes he'll guide you into all truth

About God, his nature and his ways

When the helper comes he'll guide you into all truth

About the planet, respect and preservation

When the helper comes he'll guide you into all truth

About patience, perseverance and peace.

John 14 v 16-17

52. *Who*

Who do you say that I am?
Some say John the Baptist, or Elijah
Who do you say that I am?
Some say a great teacher
Who do you say that I am?
Some say a good man
Who do you say that I am?
Some say the Messiah, the Son of God
Who do you say that I am?
Some say they don't know
Who do you say that I am?
Some say they're not sure
Who do you say that I am?
Some say they'd like to know
Who do you say that I am?
Some say they've changed their mind
Who do you say that I am?
Some say the image of the invisible God
Who do you say that I am?

Mark 8 v 29

53. *I Am*

I am the way, the truth and the life

I am alpha and omega, the beginning and the end

I am the king of glory and a man of sorrows

I am trustworthy, reliable, a solid foundation

I am stability, energy, joy and understanding

I am kindness and compassion, a friend to the lonely

I am with the poor, the broken, the lost and afraid

With the winners and losers, the strong and the weak

I am restraint and passion, self-control and zest

I am meaning, purpose, direction and hope

I am the bread of life, another kind of food and drink

I am reason and science, art and imagination

I am insight, design, welcome and acceptance

I always have been and always will be

I am.

John 14 v 6

54. *Follow Me*

Follow me and I will make you fishers of men

Follow me and I will make you searchers and rescuers

Encouragers of people

Fighters for justice

Rattlers of cages

Wrestlers with truth

Rockers of boats

Visionaries for the lost

Mouths for the voiceless

Hope for the hopeless

Light for those who sit in darkness

Smilers amongst the frowning

Listeners amongst the noise

Shoulders for those who cry

Strength for the weak

Do-ers of small significant things

Truth-bearers amongst the spin

Follow me and it won't be easy, it will cost

But I will be with you, wherever you go.

Mark 1 v 17

55. *A-Z*

Alpha and Omega

The beginning and the end

The A-Z of life

Start to finish

The big bang theory to the last day
predictions

Old earth to new one

Spiritually blind to eyes opened

Alpha and Omega

In the large details and the small

In the months and the moments

In the huge happenings and the insignificant
ones

Everywhere, anywhere, somewhere and right
here

Alpha and Omega

The beginning and the end.

Numbers 6 vv 24-26

56. *Embracing*

When Isaac sees his brother Jacob
He runs and throws his arms around him
Though the two have fallen out
He runs and throws his arms around him
He digs deep and finds forgiveness
He runs and throws his arms around him
When the father sees his son limping home
He runs and throws his arms around him
To protect him from the stones of others
He runs and throws his arms around him
To absorb any insults hurled at his child
He runs and throws his arms around him
He digs deep and finds forgiveness
He runs and throws his arms around him
To welcome him home, and say I love you
He runs and throws his arms around him
Like a mother hen, shielding her chicks from harm
He runs and throws his arms around him
It's a story that plays out every day
He runs and throws his arms around us
He digs deep and finds forgiveness

He runs and throws his arms around us
As we limp home day after day
He runs and throws his arms around us.

Luke 15 v 20; Genesis 33 v 4

57. *Valley*

Yea, though I walk through the valley of the shadow

You are with me

Though I walk through the valley of trouble

You are with me

Through the valley of despair

You are with me

Through the valley of doubt

You are with me

Through the valley of hunger and thirsting

You are with me

Through the valley of loss and emptiness

You are with me

Through the valley of trouble

You are with me

Through the valley of night

You are with me

Through the valley of darkness

I need not fear (though I often do) for you are with me.

Psalm 23 v 4

58. *Surely*

Jacob woke from his dream of angels and said,

'Surely God is in this place and I never knew it.'

He was on the run and thought he was alone

'Surely God is in this place and I never knew it.'

When I walk down the street at times something reminds me

'Surely God is in this place and I never knew it.'

When I sail close to the wind and founder I'm reminded

'Surely God is in this place and I never knew it.'

When I'm wandering in the darkness, lost again in despair

'Surely God is in this place and I never knew it.'

When we find ourselves up against a wall, cornered by life

'Surely God is in this place and we never knew it.'

When we feel alone and rejected and we need a friend

'Surely God is in this place and I never knew it.'

When we hurl ourselves towards temptation and danger

'Surely God is in this place and we never knew it.'

When we box God and confine him to heaven

'Surely God is in this place and we never knew it.'

When the pub's almost full and the church almost empty

'Surely God is in this place and we never knew it.'

And as a carpenter dies in shame and rejection, abandoned by the world

'Surely God is in this place and we never knew it.'

Genesis 28 v 16; Psalm 139 v 7

59. *Blessing*

May the Lord Bless you and keep you

May he call you and send you

The Lord make his face to shine upon you

May he comfort and inspire you

The Lord be gracious to you

May he unsettle and encourage you

The Lord lift up the light of his countenance upon you

May he affirm and challenge you

The Lord give you his peace

May he call you and send you

To do those good things that only you can do.

Numbers 6 vv 24-26

60. *Money-love*

The love of money

Causes people to use others

The love of money

Makes us crave for more

Money-love

Drives destructive habits

Money-love

Hardens hearts and stubborns wills

Money-love

Misleads and misguides those in authority

Money-love

Makes us believe more is better

Money-love

Makes us try and serve two masters

Money-love

Is the enemy of compassion

Money-love

Is the root of all evil.

1 Timothy 6 v 10

61. *Movie*

If the Bible were a movie

It would be a rom-com, a thriller, an action adventure and a mystery

If the Bible were a movie

It would be a mixture of historical drama and futuristic sci-fi

If the Bible were a movie

At times it would be enthralling and gripping, at other times complex and hard to follow

If the Bible were a movie

It would stir us, shake us, move and disturb us, make us laugh, cry, believe and question

If the Bible were a movie

The sequels would feature every day, played out in the lives of the viewers

If the Bible were a movie

We could watch it a thousand times and still see moments we had missed

If the Bible were a movie

How many would take time to see it?

2 Timothy 3 v 16

62. *Waters*

He leads me beside still waters

He calls me to stop for a moment and rest

He leads me beside still waters

He sees the stressing out and the fraying ends

He leads me beside still waters

The candle burning at both ends

He leads me beside still waters

The core of our being stretched to its limits

He leads me beside still waters

Just for a moment to catch my breath

He leads me beside still waters

Just for two seconds to renew my strength

He leads me beside still waters.

Psalm 23 vv 2-3

63. *In Vain?*

If the Lord does not build the house do the builders work in vain?

If the Lord does not watch over the city do the guards stand in vain?

If the Lord does not guide our steps do we walk in vain?

If the Lord doesn't inhabit our churches do we worship in vain?

If the Lord doesn't stir our hearts is our passion all in vain?

If the Lord doesn't renew our strength will our energy be spent in vain?

If the Lord doesn't inspire our thinking do we plan and dream in vain?

If the Lord is not in our living and being is our existence all in vain?

Psalm 127 v 1; Isaiah 40 v 31; Acts 17 v 28

64. *Why?*

Why do the nations rage and the people plot in vain?

Why does one tribe rise against another?

Why does one country want the land of another?

Why does one neighbour envy another?

Why does one family intimidate another?

Why is the news so bad all the time?

Why does justice seem to be like a fast food carton? Flimsy, easily disposable and blown about by the winds of change.

Where does this sense of injustice come from?

And what makes us ask why?

Psalm 2 v 1

65. *Encouragement*

If you have any encouragement
Then share it with each other
If you have any encouragement
Pass it on subtly or with a bang
If you have any encouragement
Say it with a smile, or a kind word
If you have any encouragement
Let it seep outwards and warm the world
If you have any encouragement
There are many ways to give it out
If you have any encouragement
Then may it strengthen and inspire you to
live differently today.

Philippians 2 v 1

66. *Blessed*

I may be blessed when I
Don't always get what I want
I may be blessed when I
Have to struggle to succeed
I may be blessed when
Expected pleasure is put on hold
I may be blessed when I
Meet God in the difficult places
I may be blessed when
It doesn't feel much like a blessing at all.

Matthew 5 vv 1-6

67. *Is*

God is

More present than I sometimes realise

God is

Sometimes only visible when I glance back over my shoulder

God is

Occasionally more obvious in the dark places

God is

Amongst the doubting, the questioning, the spiritually poor

God is

Whether I am full, empty, rich, poor, innocent, guilty, lost or found

God is

Always was, and always will be.

Matthew 5 vv 1-6; Deuteronomy 6 v 4

68. *Honour*

I will honour those who honour me
With their time and their talents
I will honour those who honour me
With their strengths and their weaknesses
I will honour those who honour me
Doing good when no one else knows
I will honour those who honour me
Patiently persevering inspiring others to do
the same
I will honour those who honour me
Holding onto truth when it's not fashionable
I will honour those who honour me
Championing love, justice and humility
I will honour those who honour me
Giving beyond what is expected
I will honour those who honour me
Going that third mile when the second is not
quite enough
I will honour those who honour me.

1 Samuel 2 v 30

69. *No One*

No one has seen God, but the only son
He has made him known
No one has seen God, but the only son
He moved into our neighbourhood
No one has seen God, but the only son
He has constructed a viewing point
No one has seen God, but the only son
He has rubbed shoulders with us
No one had seen God, but the only son
He has removed the barriers
No one had seen God, but the only son
Is a living portrait
No one has seen God, but the only son
He has made him known.

John 1 v 18

70. *Days*

On Day 1 he called out the light
On Day 2 he called out space, water & sky
On Day 3 he called out grass, plants & trees
On Day 4 he called out the sun, moon & stars
On Day 5 he called out fish and birds
On Day 6 he called out animals and people
On Day 7 he called out rest and recuperation
And so the days went by...
On Wednesday he was anointed and waiting
On Thursday he was afraid and praying
On Friday he was dying and finished
On Saturday he was dead and gone
On Sunday he was alive and well
On Monday he was out and about
Every day since he's been hard at work.

Genesis 1 & Mark 14-16

71. *In Him*

In him we love and move and have our existence

In him we walk and talk and commune with one another

In him we work and sweat and labour each day

In him we dance and sing and celebrate the good times

In him we cry and weep and struggle with the darkness

In him we rest and sleep and take those crafty catnaps

In him we buy and sell and give away to those in need

In him we have passion and love and make our romance

In him we live and move and have our existence.

Acts 17 v 28

72. *Believe*

It's not easy to believe

When you watch the news

It's not easy to believe

When things go wrong again

It's not easy to believe

When your prayers bounce off the ceiling

It's not easy to believe

When life ambushes you

But it helps when

You find there are moments of hope

It helps when

You discover others take time to pray

It helps when

Kindness invades this world again

It helps when

You know that others believe too.

73. *Speaking*

God speaks through

The beauty and the power of creation

God speaks through

The unexpected chances and coincidences

God speaks through

The good news and the kind words

God speaks through

The way we treat each other

God speaks through

The silences and the sounds

God speaks through

The moments when we have to wait

God speaks through

The moments, the days, the years.

Romans 1 v 20; Psalm 19 v 1; Job 12 vv 7-9

74. *Sheep*

One day Jesus looked at the people and saw

Sheep without a shepherd

He was stirred by the crowds who came to see him

Sheep without a shepherd

He was moved and had compassion on them

They had so many troubles and worries

Sheep without a shepherd

They often looked in the wrong places

Called on the wrong people

Sheep without a shepherd

He would keep searching for them

Never afraid of the dark or dangerous places

Sheep without a shepherd

Willing to risk everything for them

The good shepherd dying on a cross on a hill

For those *sheep without a shepherd.*

Matthew 9 v 36

75. *Excuses*

Moses, Gideon

Jonah, Jeremiah

Too young, too old

Too scared, too inexperienced

Time and again

The reluctant are called

Time and again

In spite of their excuses and weakness

Time and again

They come through

Time and again

God's power is enough.

You and I

Too young, too old

Too scared, too inexperienced

Time & again

The story goes on.

Jeremiah 1 vv 4-8; Judges 6 vv 11-16; Jonah 1 vv 1-3

76a. *Resurrection*

I am the resurrection and the life

He said, and he called Lazarus from the cold clutches of death

I am the resurrection and the life

And he tapped the boy's coffin and stirred him from that fatal slumber

I am the resurrection and the life

And he told her, 'Wake up little girl.'

I am the resurrection and the life

And he touched the untouchable people and handed them a new start

I am the resurrection and the life

And he called Zacchaeus out of his tree, and Matthew out of his tollbooth

I am the resurrection and the life

And he told the condemned woman to walk free and start again

I am the resurrection and the life

And he told the condemned man, 'Today, you'll be with me in paradise.'

I am the resurrection and the life

He says, and continues setting people free.

John 11 v 25; Luke 7 vv 20-21

76b. *Resurrection part 2*

For the rich and the powerful
I am the resurrection and the life
For the accomplished and the brave
I am the resurrection and the life
For the secure and the successful
I am the resurrection and the life
For those who don't know they need me
And for those who do
I am the resurrection and the life
For the poor, the grieving, the lost
I am the resurrection and the life
For those waiting for hope
I am the resurrection and the life
For those trapped in dead-end lives
I am the resurrection and the life
For the grateful and the giving
I am the resurrection and the life
For the tired and the troubled
I am the resurrection and the life
For the losers and the winners
I am the resurrection and the life.

John 11 v 25; Jeremiah 9 vv 23-24

77. *Boast*

Let not the wise boast in their wisdom
Or the rich in their wealth
Let not the strong boast in their power
Or the accomplished in their achievements

But instead, let them boast about this
That they know the living God
The maker of heaven and earth
The saviour of the universe

Let not the politicians boast in their successes
Or the business tycoons in their profits
Let not the famous boast in their glamour
Or the celebrities in their fame

But instead let them boast about this
That they know the living God
Born in a humble family
Worshipped by the humble and the poor

Let not any of us boast in our fragile ways
Except to boast about the humble God
Who knows us and gave everything for us.

Jeremiah 9 vv 23-24; 2 Corinthians 10 vv 17-18

78. *Living Letters*

People are living letters from God
As they watch out for one another
People are living letters from God
Parents caring for children
People are living letters from God
Folks welcoming each other
People are living letters from God
As they sit listening, nodding, taking it all in
People make the best sermons
As they pass on small, unexpected gifts
People make the best sermons
Laughing, crying, debating together
People make the best sermons
Long lost friends and everyday couples
People are living letters from God
Their actions speaking louder than words
People are living letters from God
Like God's multimedia, YouTube clips of love.

2 Corinthians 3 v 3

79. *Closer*

With every passing breath

It moves a little closer

With every blink of the eye

It comes into focus a little more

Every footstep brings it nearer

The whole world turning in the

centre of his eye

All creation gathered on its knee

The end and the beginning

Tears and laughter

Sin and redemption

Pain and healing

Death and life

Once this moment was a distant blur

Just a speck on the horizon

And no one gave it much thought

But with every breath and every blink

The day of consolation grows a little nearer.

Revelation 21

80. *God*

Bigger, more extraordinary, more caring than anything I could put on this page...

Ephesians 3 v 19

81. *Confession*

We believe in love... though we're often unloving

We believe in life... though we can sometimes look like death warmed up

We believe in truth... though we often spin those little white (?) lies

We believe in faith... though we are often full of doubt

We believe in kindness... though we can be harsh and critical

We believe in justice... even when we are unfair and selfish

We believe in generosity... though meanness can be our currency

We believe in hope, in purpose, in freedom

And though we often fail to live these out

We thank God for Jesus, who made a way through this maze

And doesn't judge, but rescues us from our contradictions.

Romans 7 vv 21-25

82. *Beginnings*

Do not despise the small beginnings
That first step
Do not despise the small beginnings
That moment of change
Do not despise the small beginnings
That sign of hope
That glimmer of light
Do not despise the small beginnings
That resolving to say no
That decision to say yes
Do not despise the small beginnings
The first brick in place
That small silent prayer
Do not despise the small beginnings
That handful of believers
That one understanding friend
Do not despise the small beginnings
That smile of encouragement
That long-held dream
Do not despise the small beginnings.

Zechariah 4 v 10

83. *Dust*

God understands how weak we are

He knows that we are dust

He is slow to anger, seeing behind and beyond our mistakes

He knows that we are dust

Like a good parent patiently caring for their children

He knows that we are dust

He is full of extraordinary kindness and compassion

He knows that we are dust

He knows our foibles, our failings and our quirks

He knows that we are dust

He will not give up on us, even though we give up on ourselves

He knows that we are dust.

Psalm 103 vv 13-14

84. *Kingdom*

Remember me, when you come into your kingdom

The kind of words many of us mutter, when we feel all is lost

Remember me, when you come into your kingdom

The kind of 'clutching at straw' words

Remember me, when you come into your kingdom

When we're up against the wall

When we've lost our reference points

Remember me, when you come into your kingdom

When all the faith we once had has vanished

When hope is gone, and we feel lost and alone

Remember me, when you come into your kingdom

Abandoned by friends and those we trusted

Remember me, when you come into your kingdom.

Luke 23 vv 40-42

85. *Abandoned* (Kingdom 2)

Remember me, when you come into your kingdom

He's dying, lost, alone, abandoned by friends and bereft of his father

Remember me, when you come into your kingdom

The words come at him from the guy dying next to him

Remember me, when you come into your kingdom

They touch him like a warm hand on the shoulder

It's not the end, he's a king, with a kingdom

Remember me…

Unexpected encouragement, from an unexpected source

And so… one desperate man encourages another

Remember me…

The Man of God, knowing what it is to be desperate, alone, lost, in despair

Remember me, when you come into your kingdom.

Luke 23 vv 40-42

86. *Bitter/Sweet*

John took the scroll from the angel and ate it
Sweet to the taste, but bitter as well
The word of God, comforting and disturbing
Sweet to the taste, but bitter as well
Affirming and accepting, shaking us up
Calling us on, helping us change
Sweet to the taste, but bitter as well
The presence of God in a place of exile
The words of life, the message of
transformation
Sweet to the taste, but bitter as well
No quick fix, no easy option
The peace of God, for a world at war with
itself
Sweet to the taste, but bitter as well
'Take up your cross,' he says, 'my burden is
easy'
In the place of exile, the presence of God
Sweet to the taste, but bitter as well.

Revelation 10 vv 8-10

87. *Depths*

Even in the depths, your hand will guide us
In the grimmest of places, you'll still be there
No reservations, no fear of the dark
We can run and hide, you'll still be there.

Night or day, hope or gloom
Cheer or sorrow, rain or shine
Even in the place we call God-forsaken
Even in the depths, you'll still be there.

Awake or asleep, tossing and turning
Calling on your name, or turning our backs
Sinking or swimming, heads full of trouble
Even in the depths, you'll still be there.

Psalm 139 vv 7-12

88. *Sustenance*

He took bread and wine and said, 'Eat and drink and remember'
Remember the man who made bread and wine for others
Remember the man who poured himself out

He took bread and wine and said, 'Eat and drink and remember'
Remember the man, his life, death and new life

His compassion, laughter, courage, hope, vulnerability, integrity, tears and honesty
He took bread and wine and said, 'Eat and drink and remember'
Remember the stories he told and the people he met
The unlikely friends he made and the generous welcome he gave
He took bread and wine and said, 'Eat and drink and remember'

Remember the fresh start, the new life, the chance to start again
Remember the invitation, remember the reason, remember and look forward
He took bread and wine and said, 'Eat and drink and remember'.

Matthew 26 vv 26-28

89. *Seeking*

You will seek me and find me
When you seek me with all your heart
In the run of the mill
And extraordinary moments
You will seek me and find me
In the Sunday worship
On a Monday morning
You will seek me and find me
In the repetitive chores
In the moments of glory
You will seek me and find me
In the sunsets and rainbows
In the gutters and alleys
You will seek me and find me
In the hurting and weak
In the triumphs and victories
You will seek me and find me
In the laughter and hope
In the struggles and doubts
You will seek me and find me
In the running and hiding
In facing the truth
You will seek me and find me
When you seek me with all your heart.

Jeremiah 29 v 13

90. *Rescue*

Lead us not into temptation, but deliver us from evil

Temptation and evil, sometimes going hand in hand

Dark soul mates, desire resulting in some kind of small destruction

Lead us not into temptation, but deliver us from evil

Doors to dark satisfaction and corridors of danger

Rescue us from this entrapment, this caustic cause and effect

Lead us not into temptation, but deliver us from evil

So many sweet subtle traps, so many glittering cages

Sugar-coated icebergs, waiting in the waters of temptation and catastrophy

Lead us not into temptation, but deliver us from evil

We struggle, we wrestle, we lose and we win

Who will rescue us from this conflicted state?

Thank God for the man from Nazareth

Thank God for forgiveness and freedom

Day after day after day…

Matthew 6 v 13

91. *The Peace of God*

May the peace of God enrich your hearts and minds

In the battles of the day and the anxieties of the night

May the peace of God enrich your hearts and minds

When folks are unreasonable and circumstances challenge you

May the peace of God enhance your hearts and minds

When those you love misunderstand and fail to appreciate

When the pressure's too great and threatens to overwhelm you

May the peace of God enrich your hearts and minds

When mountains and mole hills all look alike

May the peace of God enrich your hearts and minds

Because of Jesus, and his extraordinary compassion

May the peace of God enrich your hearts and minds.

Philippians 4 v 7

92. **My Spirit Rejoices**

When I hear the sound of voices praising your name

My soul magnifies the Lord, and my spirit rejoices in God my Saviour

When I see compassion and kindness at work in the world

My soul magnifies the Lord, and my spirit rejoices in God my Saviour

When I sense your presence in the outworking of the day

My soul magnifies the Lord, and my spirit rejoices in God my Saviour

When you help me to keep going, though I want to give up

My soul magnifies the Lord, and my spirit rejoices in God my Saviour

When I glimpse your creativity in the wonder of the world

My soul magnifies the Lord, and my spirit rejoices in God my Saviour

When moments of holiness shine like diamonds in the dark

My soul magnifies the Lord, and my spirit rejoices in God my Saviour

When I remind myself of your goodness and your care for us

My soul magnifies the Lord, and my spirit rejoices in God my Saviour

When I look at the vast night sky, and realise you know my name

My soul magnifies the Lord, and my spirit rejoices in God my Saviour

When I revisit the child, placed in that manger

My soul magnifies the Lord, and my spirit rejoices in God my Saviour.

Luke 1:46b

93. *Love, Walk, Live*

Act justly
Love mercy
Walk humbly
Act kindly
Love justice
Nurture humility.

Lean towards the right thing
Embrace compassion
Do your best to shun pride
Offer hope
Let your light shine
No matter how small.

Try and live with integrity
Watch out for one other
Keep walking, limping
Running or stumbling
With your God.

Micah 6 v 8

94. *Loaves*

The young boy came to Jesus, offering his five loaves and two fish

She brought her singing voice

He brought his gift of the gab

He brought his love of art

She brought her passion for sport

They brought their love of cooking

Others brought their love of nature

He brought his quiet ways

She brought her boisterous ones

They brought their hope and laughter

Others brought their tears and compassion

The young boy came to Jesus, offering his five loaves and two fish

And Jesus took them

Those sandwiches and snacks

Blessed them and multiplied the gifts.

John 6 vv 7-12

95. *XOXO*

I have loved you with an everlasting love
Not a *Mars Bar* kind of love
Not a new pair of shoes kind of affection
Not a 'woo-you' greeting on a bit of spam
I have loved you with an everlasting love
Nothing passing or flimsy
Nothing frivolous or transient
Nothing that will ever come to nothing
I have loved you with an everlasting love
Endless and inexhaustible
Supreme and limitless
Impossible to deplete
I have loved you with an everlasting love
Though you may struggle to sense it
Wrestle to believe it
And rebel against it sometimes
I have loved you with an everlasting love
Sealed with a single, sacrificial X
On a dark and transforming hillside
More than hugs and kisses
I have loved you with an everlasting love.

Jeremiah 31 v 3

96. *Praise!*

Praise the LORD!
Praise the LORD from the heavens; praise him in the heights!

Praise him on the earth below.

Praise him in the home and at church

Praise him in the park and on the pavement

Climbing and walking, running and standing still

Praise him on the sports pitch and in the cinema

Praise him at school and at work

When the sun shines and when it doesn't

Praise him in the minutes and the years

When the minutes feel like years and the years feel like minutes

Praise him with others, praise him alone

Praise him aloud, with shouts and whispers

Praise him in silence, from the quiet corners of your being

Praise him in the bustle and the rush of each passing day

Praise him here, there and everywhere.

Praise the LORD!
Praise the LORD from the heavens; praise him in the heights!

Praise him on the earth below.

Psalm 148

97. *Mindful of Us*

When I look at your heavens, the work of your fingers

When I see the moon and the stars that you have established

What are human beings that you are mindful of them, ordinary people that you care for us?

When I look at the snow-smeared mountains, massive and imposing

When I see the raging oceans and the depths still waiting to be discovered

What are human beings that you are mindful of them, ordinary people that you care for us?

When I wonder at the intricate science of creation

And the fragile features of this world

What are human beings that you are mindful of them, ordinary people that you care for us?

When I hear about the news, about a planet so often at war with itself

When I have to face another day, another week, another month, of duty and difficulty

What are human beings that you are mindful of them, ordinary people that you care for us?

When I realise that I still have so much to learn

When I find again that I do not have all the answers

What are human beings that you are mindful of them, ordinary people that you care for us?

When I remember Jesus, his humility and compassion

When I look again on that darkened cross

What are human beings that you are mindful of them, ordinary people that you care for us?

When I look at the moon and the stars, the work of your fingers,

The glory of your presence, writ large in the heavens

What are human beings that you are mindful of them, ordinary people that you care for us?

Psalm 8 vv 3-9

98. *OMG*

Oh my God, so many say, in times of crisis,
pain or shock

*The words f*alling easily without much
thought or taking stock

Oh my God, on social media, trending
through the day

While billions round the world make a
sacrifice to pray.

Oh my God your name goes viral by the
minute, by the hour

Not so much a heartfelt prayer, but snack
food with little power

Oh my God, the cry may slip from a million
lips tonight

And for some who talk or text it won't be
crass or trite.

Oh my God holds a meaning, etched on a
cross of blood

Where sweat and death and tears have
changed the world for good.

Oh my God, do you flinch, or shed a tortured tear,

For every O, every M and every G that you hear?

Do you ever get hardened to the never-ending hail?

Or does each one pierce your being like another Roman nail?

Oh my God, the psalmist cries, his anguish bursting from his core

He means his OMG like he never did before

He has a God who understands, knows the meaning of the words -

The cry of joy, the wail of pain and the terror of the years.

OMG we may cry - for some it's merely punctuation

But for others it's a treasured song, a prayer of adulation.

Psalm 22 v 1- 5 & Matthew 27 vv 45-46

99. *Comfort*

In times of trouble, you are our comfort and our strength

When hope eludes us and fear casts a long shadow

You are our comfort and our strength

When the future is uncertain and the way unclear

You are our comfort and our strength

When doubts fly like arrows, piercing all that is precious

You are our comfort and our strength

When today is difficult and tomorrow looks no better

In times of trouble, stress or panic, you are our comfort and our strength.

Psalm 46 v 1

100. *Salvation*

The Lord God is my strength and my might;
he has become my salvation.

I look to him for the energy to make it
through this day

For the help to get through the tough
moments

For the courage to be faithful and honest

For the inspiration to keep going

For the compassion to care for others

The Lord God is my strength and my might;
he has become my salvation.

I look to him for hope when disappointment
occurs

And for the wisdom to see beyond the
surface

For the patience when *that thing* occurs yet
again

For the good humour to smile and laugh

And for the light heart to not take myself too
seriously

The Lord God is my strength and my might;
he has become my salvation.

Psalm 118 v 14

101. *My Sheep*

My sheep hear my voice

Though the listening can be hard

My sheep hear my voice

Though so many voices clamour for attention

My sheep hear my voice

Sometimes in the loneliness of the longest night

At times in the heat of the day

My sheep hear my voice

In the shadows and the silhouettes

In the worship and the work

My sheep hear my voice

In the quiet and the calm

In the storms and the clamouring

My sheep hear my voice

In the words of the prophets and the letters of Paul

In the tales from the gospels and the writings of Moses

My sheep hear my voice

In the kindness of others and the smiles of strangers

In the moments of strength and the times of
weariness

My sheep hear my voice

In the gaps and the moments

In the unexpected silence

My sheep hear my voice.

John 10 v 27

102. *Treasure*

Mary treasured all these words and pondered them in her heart:

The message of the angel, 'Don't be afraid, you are highly favoured.'

Mary treasured all these words and pondered them in her heart:

The words of the shepherds, 'Peace on earth, goodwill to all.'

Mary treasured all these words and pondered them in her heart:

The gifts from the wise men, 'Gold for a king, incense for a God.'

The prophecy of Simeon, 'This child will be the rising and falling of many.'

Mary treasured all these words and pondered them in her heart:

The vision of the prophets, 'The people walking in darkness have seen a great light.'

The song of her cousin, 'You are blessed above all, and so is your child.'

Mary treasured all these words and pondered them in her heart:

The promise of hope, 'Unto us a child is born, and he will be called wonderful, counsellor, prince of peace, mighty God.'

Mary treasured all these words and pondered them in her heart.

Luke 2:19

103. *When*

When you pass through the deep waters
And through the raging rivers
They shall not overwhelm you
When you walk through the fire
You shall not be burned
I will be with you. I have called you by name.

When the waters of fear lap at the doors of
your life
When the rivers of terror threaten to
overwhelm you
When the fire of confusion and the flames of
despair scorch your purpose
I will be with you. I have called you by name.

When the storms of life and the tremors of
day-to-day living shake everything
When the morbid drizzle of weariness just
won't let up
When the battering winds of secularism hit
you once again
I will be with you. I have called you by name.

When the smog of disunity blocks your way forward

When the clouds of backbiting and gossip hang heavy in the air

When the thunderous cracks of cynicism resound once again

I will be with you. I have called you by name.

Isaiah 43 v 2

104. *Prepare the Way of the Lord*

Prepare the way of the Lord

Make his paths straight, and honour his name

Prepare the way of the Lord

With courage and kindness, honesty and hope

Prepare the way of the Lord

With much strength or little, whatever you have

With a smile, a helping hand, and a listening ear

Prepare the way of the Lord

With words of vision and encouragement, challenge and direction

With acts of compassion, and generous hearts

Prepare the way of the Lord

For the young, the old, and all in between

Though the world seems against you, and the road may be hard

Prepare the way of the Lord

Make his paths straight, and honour his name

Prepare the way of the Lord.

Malachi 3 v 1 & John 3 v 27

105. *139*

Lord, we are wonderful and complex

Glorious and grubby

Magnificent and moaning

Hopeful yet heretical

Troubled and trusting

Faithful and forgetful

Spiritual and secular

Lord, we are wonderful and complex

With hungry hearts and feet of clay

Slipping and sliding as we look to the stars

Stubbing our toes as we tread on sacred ground

Giving and grabbing, generous and greedy

Loving but loathing, caring but criticising

Capable of good and bad, right and wrong

Doing at times what we don't want to do

Lord, we are wonderful and complex

And you understand

You see us when we sit and when we stand, when we go out and return

In the light and the dark, in our laughter and despair
When we walk with you, and when we don't
Forgive us, renew us, refresh and inspire us
Lord, we are wonderful and complex.

Psalm 139 & Psalm 51 vv 1-17

106. *Love Is*

Love is patient and kind

It is not jealous or conceited or proud

Love is difficult

Often calling to us when we are busy

Love is in the small things

It can feel insignificant, too small to count

Love rarely makes headlines

Yet it can change someone's world

Love goes against the flow

Cuts against the grain, points to the narrow
road

Love can feel like trudging uphill

Battling against the wind, walking a lonely
path

But God is love

And God has walked these ways

Trudged up that hill, walked that path

Love is pinned on a skyline

Nailed to a darkened, belittled cross

Love changes the world

One heartbeat, one sacrifice at a time.

1 Corinthians 13

107. *Presence*

There is nowhere I can go and lose your
presence
The dark and the light are the same to you
Darkness is not dark, night and day are the
same
You're not afraid of the shadows or the
gloom

There is nowhere I can go and lose your
presence
Nowhere I can step, where you've not
stepped before
Nowhere too grim, too ugly or god-forsaken
Nowhere to dangerous or dull for you

There is nowhere I can go and lose your
presence
If I flew to the furthest point on the horizon
To the heights or the depths, mountains or
valleys
Your hand will be there to comfort and guide

In the roar of traffic or the loneliness that
lingers
In the sacred and secular, the rich and the
poor

There is nowhere I can go and lose your presence
You find me in an instant - you're already there.

Psalm 139 vv 1-18

108. *No Longer Despised*

You shall no longer be called despised
Or seen as forsaken
For the Lord delights in you.
Those who are struggling to pay their way
Those who worry about the future
You shall no longer be called despised
Or seen as forsaken
For the Lord delights in you.

Those who are not listed amongst the great
and the good
Those who will never make the celebrity a-list
You shall no longer be called despised
Or seen as forsaken
For the Lord delights in you.
Those who feel shunned and ignored
Those who struggle to get by each day
You shall no longer be called despised
Or seen as forsaken
For the Lord delights in you.

Those whose hopes have been crushed
Those whose dreams were dashed by life

You shall no longer be called despised

Or seen as forsaken

For the Lord delights in you.

Isaiah 62 v 4

109. *Reminders*

The heavens paint a picture of the glory of
God
Hope-stained hands streak the endless
canvass
The sun in its splendour, daubs another
sunset
Celestial colours on the sprawling sky.

Seraphic brushstrokes smear the horizon
With hues and shades that beckon to us
Our eyes and minds drawn to another
dimension
Reminders that we are not here alone.

The subtle shading from the great 'I Am'
A divine text message from the great beyond
Signs of his presence when loneliness lurks
The hope of bright morning, after the fear of
the dark
The heavens paint a picture of the glory of
God
Reminders that we are not here alone.

Psalm 19

110. *Help*

When we have spent our energy and run out of ideas

When we have tried so hard and yet still fall short

When our vision has gone up in smoke again

When our plans have not succeeded as they should

Help us Lord.

When you come to us by the water's edge

When you ask us to turn and try once more

When you suggest that we have one more go (and our pride battles for supremacy)

When it feels such an effort to push the boat out again

Help us Lord.

When that deep water seems deeper than ever

When the rowing is harder than it really should be

When it's hard to believe this effort will be worth it

When it seems unfair that we should have to try once more

Help us Lord.

When we realise that we are weaker than you

When we sense that you are holier than us

When we get the notion that you have made things happen

When we fall on our knees in weakness and praise

Help us Lord.

Luke 5 vv 1-9

111. *Longing*

As Jesus neared Jerusalem his heart fractured
'How long I've been waiting to draw my
people close to me ...'

As he told his tales of the kingdom
As he washed the feet of his friends
As he rode into Jerusalem, a humble king
As he spent energy on the lowly and unloved
'How long I've been waiting to draw my
people close to me ...'

As he reached out to the oppressed and the
oppressors
As he went willingly with those who had
come to arrest him
As he stood before the powerful men of his
day
As he offered his hands to those unmerciful
nails
'How long I've been waiting to draw my
people close to me ...'

As the terror of isolation gripped the core of
his being

As he threw his head to the skies and gasped
his last

As he woke from death and the earth
shuddered

As he walked back into the lives of friends
and others

'How long I've been waiting to draw my
people close to me …'

As he prays for us, each and every day

As he looks on the world, wrestling and
broken

As he hears the cries of a battered creation

As he waits for us to lift our eyes to him

'How long I've been waiting to draw my
people close to me …'

As Jesus neared Jerusalem his heart fractured

'How often I've longed to gather my people
together

As a hen gathers her brood under her
wings…'

Luke 13 v 34

112. *Shelter*

Those who live in the shelter of the Most High

Those who abide in the shadow of the Almighty

Will say to the LORD, "My refuge and my fortress; my God, in whom I trust."

Those who call for help in times of trouble

Those who seek strength to make it through another day

Those who wrestle to remain calm and compassionate

Will say to the LORD, "My refuge and my fortress; my God, in whom I trust."

Those who need courage to stand up for truth

Those who require fresh purpose when the well has run dry

Those who seek solace from the fast lanes of life

Will say to the LORD, "My refuge and my fortress; my God, in whom I trust."

Those who dig deep to keep changing the situation

Those who need shelter when another storm rages

Those who live in the shadow of the Most High

Will say to the LORD, "My refuge and my fortress; my God, in whom I trust."

Psalm 91

113. *Doves, Ravens, Eagles & Hens*

Once a raven took to flight, went out from
Noah's hand

Left the ark, and braved the skies, in a
desperate bid for land.

It returned empty.

It later brought a clutch of food gripped
within its beak

Fed a prophet called Elijah, stranded by a
dying creek.

It saved his life.

Years went by then one bright day it was
spotted in the air

When a man from Galilee saw a sign of God's
good care.

'Think on it,' he said.

A dove then left the grip of Noah on his
behemoth boat

It found new life, brought back a sign for
those adrift, afloat.

Hope. A new start.

A psalm writer prayed for wings, for freedom
like that dove

To leave behind the pressure, escape the push and shove.

His prayer is ours.

Then one day at the Jordan - a dove, a voice, a sign

As heaven called with thunder, 'This boy is loved, he's mine.

Listen to him.'

Signs in the sky, wings and beaks, tales of other things

Those waiting on the hope of God, soar on eagles' wings .

Walking, running, not fainting.

The kingdom like a rampant weed, where birds will come and nest

Mustard from a tiny seed, the kind we might reject.

Not as we expect.

As the son of man neared his time, he imagined a mother hen

Gathering chicks, saved from fire, giving life and breath to them.

The carpenter hammered to death.

Like the Phoenix rising once again, from the ash of hate and fear

There's an open tomb and a broken seal, and a gardener waiting near.

The carpenter awakes.

For life, for people, for planets and stars, for creatures and the birds

A new dawn breaks, a man walks free, splintering death's dark curse.

He smiles.

As in the beginning, when the world awoke, and birds first filled the planet

So there'll be a whole new start, and the one who once began it

Will live with us.

Forever.

Genesis 8 vv 6-12, 1 Kings 17 vv 2-6, Psalm 55 vv 4-7
Luke 3 vv 20-22, Isaiah 40 vv 29-31, Luke 13 vv 34-35
Luke 13 v 19, John 20 vv 11-18, Revelation 21 vv 1-5

114. *The One*

Let the same mind be in you that was in Christ Jesus, the One, the living word, there at the beginning, the source of life and creation.

Though he was God, he didn't regard equality with God as something to be exploited.

He didn't grab at power, or hold onto pride, but instead humbled himself, let go and emptied himself, taking the form of a slave, being born in human likeness.

Living in a humble community, in a country under oppression, he learnt his father's trade, sweated and toiled, studied and grew, laughed and cried. Before trekking into the wilderness, where he was tested, tried and tempted. Then, for three full years, he brought life and light to those living in the shadow of death.

And being found in human form, he humbled himself and became obedient to the point of death - even death on a cross. That cruel criminal punishment, a slave's execution; after a life of service and hope, compassion and washing feet.

Therefore God highly exalted him and gave him the name that is above every name, so that at the name of Jesus every knee should bend, in heaven and on earth and under the earth. The whole of creation acknowledging the glory, the wonder, the unique nature and inexpressible brilliance of the Man of Sorrows, the Son of God, the Alpha and Omega. Every tongue confessing that Jesus Christ is Lord, to the glory of God the Father.

Philippians 2 vv 5-11

115. *The Former Things*

Do not remember the former things, or consider the things of old.

But it's not that easy Lord, some of us don't want to let go of the former things

Some of us can't let go

And for some of us times were so much better back then.

Do not remember the former things, or consider the things of old.
Lord, some of us want to let go, but others won't let us

For some of us those were the glory days and the flowers have long-since faded

And some of us have lost our way and no longer have the strength.

I will make a way in the wilderness and rivers in the desert.
Some of us look at these promises like children gazing through shop windows

Our noses pressed to the glass, longing and hoping

Desperate for a new thing, for a way through this wilderness.

I will make a way in the wilderness and rivers in the desert.

Some of us have been in this desert so long it's starting to look like home

We've forgotten we're travellers

We swapped our tents for mobile homes, and our mobile homes for bricks and mortar.

Today is a new day, a voice whispers

A still small voice calls amidst the thunder

I am the God of *I am*. The God of now. Present in the present.

I will help you take the steps you need today, in order to move towards tomorrow.

Do not remember the former things, or consider the things of old.

I will make a way in the wilderness and rivers in the desert.

I am about to do a new thing, do you perceive it?

Isaiah 43 vv 18-19

116. *Fresh Start*

Happy are those whose wrongdoing is forgiven, whose faults are taken care of

Those who are being released from past failure, whose slates are wiped clean

Happy are those who tell God about their mistakes and problems, who know they need him

Those who find that God is gracious and kind, slow to anger and rich in love

Happy are those who find they can bring their frailties and weaknesses, missteps and mishaps to God

Those who know the shackles of their past are broken

Happy are those who are able to swap pride for humility

Those who discover that Jesus gave himself – not because people deserve it, because people need it

Happy are those who find a fresh start in the man from Nazareth.

Psalm 32

117. *Bread and Wine*

Jesus took some bread and tore it in pieces

Then he lifted the cup and held it up

'Take this bread,' he said

'Drink this wine

My body

My blood

My life broken for you and poured out for all...'

That servant heart shattered and dispersed amongst us

That life for the world

That living word, distributed around the universe

His strength, his honour, his energy and compassion

Given, offered, laid bare for us

Waiting for the taking

For the eating and drinking.

'Do this and remember me,' he said,

'Celebrate my life, my death, my resurrection

The new agreement between the creator and his creation

Eat and drink, remember and remind one another

Take this bread,' he said

'And drink this wine.'

And so we come together

As we are

Strong and weak, clear-sighted and muddled, hungry and thirsty

For answers, for solutions, for a way forward, for righteousness

In faith, hope, and love.

Matthew 26 vv 26-29

118. **The Bible**

The Bible - it's a world within a world, a difficult, hopeful, untamed land, another dimension where time moves differently. It's a place of stories, struggles, faith, doubt, wonder, hope, loss, despair and healing. One time zone pauses as another opens up, the pages of history and poetry flicker past in the candlelight of our soul-searching. It's frustrating, bewildering, infuriating, inspiring, heart-warming and mind-expanding. A stick jammed in the spokes of the system. A giant-slaying, beast-destroying, life-transforming work, a place where holiness and hope embrace. A home for pilgrims and wanderers, stragglers and wayfarers.

Genesis 1 - Revelation 22

119. *Chosen*

As they were on the mountain a cloud came down.

And a voice declared,

'This is my beloved son. The chosen one. Listen to him.'

If we had eyes to see that mountain cloud, would it be present again?

In our streets and homes

At school, at work, and in the places of unemployment

In the churches and pubs

In the sports stadiums and cinemas.

And would we hear that voice saying,

'These are my children, my beloved sons and daughters. Chosen ones.'

And though this mountain cloud may not be visible,

The voice may sometimes whisper to us,

In the songs and the silence

In the busyness and bustle

In the smiles of others

In the compassion of those who care

'You are my child, my beloved one. Chosen.'

Luke 9 vv 34-35

120. *Psalm 51*

Have mercy on us, O Lord

According to your incomparable,
extraordinary love
You know about our wrongs and our mistakes
and our brokenness.

Cleanse us through and through, renew us,
and revive us

Help us to forgive ourselves, for we are
aware of our flaws and frailties

Save us from false guilt, and from putting
ourselves down.

We get things wrong, we know this, and we
hurt you and others

We are people with soiled hands and feet of
clay

Capable of great things, and gruesome things

Capable of healing and harm.

You desire the best for us, you offer us a
hope and a future

Help us to face the truth about ourselves, and
about you

And as we do this we offer you our failures and successes

Our weakness and strengths, our dreams and nightmares.

You are not fooled, you see us as we are

And you have the kind of compassion that we can only imagine

So please, refresh us, cleanse us, rebuild our confidence, and renew our faith

And enable us to act honestly, to care deeply, and to walk humbly with you

Today and each day

In the name of your son Jesus,

Amen.

Psalm 51

121. *PTL*

Praise the Lord!

Praise Him in the streets and the city

Praise him in the towns and the villages

Praise him in the pubs and the churches

In the sports stadiums and back gardens

Praise him in the lounge and the kitchen

In the bathroom and the hallway

Praise him when the sun shines and when the rain falls

Praise him with a smile and with tears

In the mountains and the valleys and the plains in between

Praise him with your own voice, in your own way

Praise him with half a breath or a lungful of shouting

Sitting still or running a marathon

Praise him with a simple lifting of your eyes

Or with an ear splitting roar

With a shout of praise or a cry of anguish

With a whispered plea or a gentle smile

Praise him with words, thoughts, songs and actions

In your work, leisure, competition, kindness, service and sacrifices

Praise him with the small things and the great

Praise him as you help others

Praise him in those unseen things you do

Praise him as you do what you do best

And by doing the difficult things

Praise him.

Psalm 150

122. *In Disguise*

While they were walking together he drew near
In disguise, quietly listening, unnoticed for a time.
While they were talking together he came alongside
In disguise, available, asking what they were discussing.

'Don't you know?' they said, 'are you oblivious?'
He smiled, 'Tell me about it,' he said.
And so they did, as they walked together
And he quietly listened, in disguise, taking it all in.

And so they talked and he listened
Nodding at news he already knew
Already understood on a much deeper level,
And when they had finished he spoke, in disguise.

And he took them back in time,
Back through history and the prophets,

Back through pain and trouble and longing,
Back to the dawning of a plan.

And so they stopped for food and he broke
bread,
As he had done with them only days before.
He lifted the bread in disguise
And lowered it as Jesus of Nazareth, the
resurrected one.

And as their eyes were opened
He disappeared. No more need for disguise
No more need to be there in that place.
And so they ran back to their friends.

No more escaping, no more fleeing.
And as they told their story he drew near
again.
And so it is today, Jesus of Nazareth often
walks close,
Resurrected, listening, understanding,
available.
In disguise.

Luke 24 vv 13-34

And Finally 3 Extras: *On The Beach*

When Jesus met Peter on that beach
After Peter had denied knowing him three times
Jesus didn't
Confront him and make him feel small
Hold a grudge for years
Ask him to grovel and plead in the sand
Order him to work hard for his forgiveness.

When Peter met Jesus on that beach
After he had denied knowing him three times
Jesus asked him three times
'Do you love me?'
And then he gave him a new start
A fresh beginning
'Come, be my disciple,' he said, 'follow me.'

When we meet Jesus each morning
After another yesterday of ups and downs
Jesus doesn't
Confront us and make us feel small
Hold a grudge for years
Ask us to grovel and plead in the sand
Order us to work hard for our forgiveness.

Instead
Jesus asks us again
'Do you love me?'
Even with the little love we have
And he offers us a new start
A fresh beginning,
'Come, be my disciple,' he says, 'follow me.'

John 21 vv 13-19

There

I was there at the start when everything began
When the lights first came on and breath came into man.
I was with you in the days that followed on from there
As things began to drift, with rebellion in the air.

I was there when the first brother killed the other one
When the stain of violence soiled the world, so much good undone.
I was there in every battle, meeting those on every side
Befriending anyone who'd notice as I crossed the great divide.

I've been there in the peace, in the failure and success
In the hopes and dreams and crashes, every mire every mess.
But I've never been there more than on the day of Roman death
When they took me, beat and nailed me, and stole my final breath.

And there in that garden, when the tomb was cracked in two
When faithful women looked for me and wondered what to do.
When life was reinvented and resurrection filled the air
The sign that I would never leave... that I would, yes...
be always there.   Joshua 1 v 9, Matthew 28 v 20

Gaps

God in the gaps
In that thin moment after breathing out
Before breathing in
In that whispery pause before the service
And the shuffling lull as it comes to an end
In the unexpected places
The un-spiritual zones
The surprising moments
The disorganised moments
The disruptive moments
In the shadowed nooks
In the dusty corners
In the cluttered places
The Monday mess
The Tuesday chores
The Wednesday work
And the Thursday thankless tasks
When everyone around is expecting something
else
God arrives
In strange disguise
In the gaps.

1 Kings 19 vv 11-12

Printed in Poland
by Amazon Fulfillment
Poland Sp. z o.o., Wrocław